PARTICLES

The Hugh MacLennan Poetry Series

Editors: Tracy Ware and Allan Hepburn
Selection Committee: Mark Abley, Donald H. Akenson,
Philip Cercone, and Joan Harcourt

TITLES IN THE SERIES

Particles

Michael Penny

McGill-Queen's University Press
Montreal & Kingston • London • Ithaca

© McGill-Queen's University Press 2011
ISBN 978-0-7735-3846-7

Legal deposit first quarter 2011
Bibliothèque nationale du Québec

Printed in Canada on acid-free paper.

McGill-Queen's University Press acknowledges the support of
the Canada Council for the Arts for our publishing program.
We also acknowledge the financial support of the Government
of Canada through the Canada Book Fund for our publishing
activities.

Library and Archives Canada Cataloguing in Publication

Penny, Michael, 1952–
    Particles / Michael Penny.

    (The Hugh MacLennan poetry series ; 23)

    Poems.
    ISBN 978-0-7735-3846-7

    I. Title. II. Series: Hugh MacLennan poetry series; 23

    PS8631.E5725P37 2011   C811'.6   C2010-906571-9

This book was typeset by Interscript in 10.5/13 Sabon.

PARTICLES

1

You are a moment
a bookmark for a time
you come back to
again and again
as it is merely you.

Use time well.
There's just enough:
No getting out of it
no gap, no going back.

Your ideas exist here
in time, that full container
which holds place and you.

2

You plan for events not yet events
until by the tipping of time
some clock is observed and met.

It's all in the numbers and hands
the work fingers do as they count
and they do count.

The work clocks do
assigning numbers to an empty continuum
fools you into thinking it makes sense.

You do this to yourself
seeking definition in all the emptiness
all those numbers all those hands.

3

You fail to endorse what might be
as what is or to observe
and observing find that it is.

A tree won't worry it exists.
It will never have that conversation with you.

You watch and note the clenched bud
the slow stretch of leaves
and then a flowering.
All that effort before the decay
into what might survive winter.

You see all this and know you have to
know, that moment of "It is."

4

This is a place
a vacuum
filled with nothing
which itself can make nothing.

There'd be pride
if there were room for it.
And expansion and contraction.

Even a vacuum has borders
the margin at which something
comes up to be something.

Because nothing cannot be
until you've drawn that line at something.

5

Draw a blank, then a line
around a blank to prove it can't be there.

Thus all the answered achievements
will be caught and let go.

Know this:

in the end there is nothing to know
nothing certain through senses
or guessing or working it out

but as the bird assumes air
as it launches itself from the nest

you are entitled to enough
to make an occupation, a life.

6

What do you do when there's millions of words
already, and thousands new each day
and sentence possibilities beyond number?

Has it all become big and complicated
enough you need all those words
to make all the sentences which are you?

Is there now so much detail
(which includes you)
that you need all those words

or are those words making details
for a universe beyond you
(which includes you)?

7

There are this many steps in a day
from the turning of the day quietly during sleep
to the sun which hauls itself up through your windows

and the house seeming to come to rest
in the middle of the sky with its heat
but still sliding step by step to make a day.

There are steps under all that light as things get done
and lists crossed off to make new lists.

And some matter and some don't.

You take all these steps
(which look like progress)
under the sliding sun.

8

The now that you're in now
is a point of no dimension
except containing all the others
as it holds your planet, galaxy
even the idea there's another now
right next door, a different room
for what it is you're thinking now.

It should be easy, limited thus
as everything collapses into
that point which now contains.

But now you're lost
as you've slipped into your past.

9

You are the centre of the universe
because everything to the right and left
is to the right and left of you

up and down and diagonals
are all you at the centre
because it all recedes from you.

Or do you sense you bring it in through
the five gates of a brain which knows what it is?

In the end, the end is the same distance
whether measured from you
left, right, up, down, or along those diagonals
which also turn out to be infinite.

10

There's a gap between where
an electron is and where it might be
and that's the only real work-place.

You occupy that office of possibility.
With what will work out for you there.

The place itself is as imaginary
as all things described.

The job description is not you;
instead, you are this to do list:

pass time; gain energy; make it matter.

And the last "to do" is yourself
that gap, your work-day, today.

11

You can escape and slide around the curve
that might be space, might be desire
both so physical, or not.

It's a matter of finding coordinates
and probabilities.
What will work.

Will your energy
(merely the mass which keeps you here)
be enough and will you survive

the actual thrill of that escape
from an atomic bond, or merely
the interference of yourself?

12

There's too much to know.
Only so much you can know.
And you can't be sure anyway.

Those are the problems: it's unfair
there's more than what's understood.

What's the use of that extra?
As it causes elements to make
compounds and vapours

which climb into clouds
you then see and can expect
rain today, but not for sure.

You can only drink it in.

13

There is a pin pricking
the sensitive skin of your finger
or what your brain says is "finger."

In that moment of steel
the whole universe is sharp
and there at that nerve.

So one bare prickle is everything
and, even absent, is still something
because nothing fails to leave a memory
as the point approaches
and you remember to flinch
at what's nothing, except it's there.

14

The universe went along OK
black holes and the matter
drawn into them and, it appears,

appearing on the other side
of that something which is nothing.
All these adjacent manifolds,

if "adjacent" has a meaning
when it's all a coherent whole
around that hole which is also the edges,

walls, the space that permits vacancy,
and then this digression
this consciousness which can do the math.

15

Where reside the things which didn't happen?
In you?

And is there an out there
where these things
can live and play out
their not having happened?

Except that now
you have given them
a place by this mere consideration.

What comes from this other place
where things take place

which don't?

16

When you look into it you start
with the individual cells, which are you.

Then you see molecules, tangled skeins
they are, but somehow knit together
as your skin and all that's inside.

And see into those molecules
atoms, small, medium, and large
but themselves made of the particles
composed from your smallest idea.

And all imbedded into emptiness
so much nothing that nothing
could describe it, even though it's you.

17

Water gives up the space of the shape
drowned in it

and the level of water amends
with gold, lead or your hand
which also tests.

Physics is correct.

You are wrong
or didn't do the math
or used the wrong variables
in this place water occupies
with all the variables water understands.

But your hand still disturbs.

18

Water makes the noise
of movement but otherwise
when quite still stands quite still.

Speaking is only another thing in motion
as words must follow other words
as water flows after water

and all this might lead somewhere
whether directed by gutter
or covering the page

which leaves so much space around
through which nothing flows
and for which you have no words.

19

The flat earth aligns its triangles
and edges into the sphere
astronomers say it must be
even if your feet know different.

There might be hills and valleys
but those are mere landscape not where you stand.

Memory has its own geography
as it delineates its countries
colouring them in so gradually.

For you to be upright
feet must find that flat surface
where earth and memory make all the difference.

20

You plant fields with stones
worship them and align them
with those other stones in the sky.

You understand the real and solid thus
mark it, record it, live from it.

And then one night
you turn toward those stones
and find crystal eyes on you
evaluative and staring
at your staring back.

The fields rest or grow grass
and take their burden lightly.

21

All the number codes work on the answer
to your hardwired need to investigate and understand.

Or, without understanding
you do it anyway
drive your car ignorant of the chemistry of petroleum

or even the million
tiny explosions you might call progress.

The nerve damage–as in
not knowing what is–is extensive.

There's no pain this way,
and also no passage
and you reach no destination.

22

And you come around the curve and crest the hill
to find the flat and straight lines and glass of a city.

Everything directed to containers
as if a rectangular cube were the shape
that recalls universes.

Or what you might hope them to be.

And, on that hill, looking down from the edge
of what is really all space flung
like a sheet in an impatient bed-maker's hands.

Get on with it.
Lie down in it.
Call it home.

23

Sometimes not staying still
creates its own turbulence

but going out avoids solitude
not itself as smooth as it might appear.

In the end whatever there is to air
it's not private, not alone.

What you breathe will carry clouds
and coughs...

and song too, and song.

So what causes that?

The singing of motion
into existence.

24

The light-bulb filament
channels its electrons
faster, faster, above your head
and the life you carry on at night.

Because it is above
you give it no thought

until that moment
of flash and dazzle
and something's gone wrong

and you know that now dark glass
like a teared-up eye once held
among other things, light.

25

Your car tires carry on their conversation
with the road's irregularities and experience
as they say: you are going there.

But your going is just today and the highway
with its signs, name, and direction goes on
in what now passes for perpetuity.

You have always come along this way
footpath, wagon trail, and now a map's broad red line
and those essential buildings.

Where is this? Where are you going?

All too hard to contemplate,
but the road's still there.

You might find it under the sun.
It likely isn't there
but there's enough light.

You keep looking
because eyes are open
because it's day under the sun.

You are a simple result
merely circumstantial perhaps
but sure it's important

or that importance will find you
perhaps while you're still searching
under the sunlight.

It's hard to organize
all your ancestors

so much is taken by other histories
and these former lives
jostling elbows out
making their space.

And this is why they end up
stacked in the shelves of your deep storage
perhaps making other generations

and unlikely histories
all merely to complete
that catalogue which lists you.

28

From above landscape shows
its construction from blocks
ranged along rivers
unable to take a straight line
except to down.

And then there's that other creation
the stepped disposal of a hillside
into a mine, the stubbly
expanse of what was forest

and then you recognize the town
square and definite
it all made.

29

So many tiny lights on the black
some unsure enough to fade and remove
their soft asterisks.

This from above.
Below
each is a world
a vocation pursued.

Night will not discourage all.
In fact it gives extra time
and a meaning
that you would not have in the sun.

Thus trying makes day again.

30

Does the seed scan the soil
for a location for roots
and the air for a space for leaves?

As it must it is finding by augury
the smallest point at which new seeds can belong.

The seed speaks thus a future language
the grammar of which gets it
to itself a season later

on which to build endless seasons
as if it under them
for its own accommodation

as empty will not labour on.

31

The pigeons bob and peck at the scattered grain
they have made their restaurant.

If it is wrong to assist pests
or decry success in this dove
which cities breed a little wild
among the traffic of foot and car
you still see something which can fly
between the smooth buildings, if startled to it.

There will always be feathers and bird shit
pressed in the pavement to remind you
that sometimes even pests fly
and you feed them, knowingly or not.

The blown pollen floats on the quiet surface
of the urban lake and oily water
solid with its abandoned bottles and bridges.

The pollen makes patterns of clump and disperse.

The concentric ripple of an underwater creature
investigates the surface.

The pollen will dampen and drown
and carp turtle or some other philosopher
will continue to know there's a surface
it can ripple for a moment but never get through.

In the end you are here
but not here, merely close.

33

There are gaps in your house that small insects
crawl through arranging their legs
inconspicuously but on your window sill.

It might be your duty–higher order of animal and all–
to take a moment and squash each small insect
as it comes to your attention.

You have this right although its legs and friends
outnumber yours, but you stop.

What would it know of its life
and its ending if you swatted it?

You would know more
and that's enough to enjoin your hand.

34

Outside is all insects.

You do not know their names
although introduced to them.

Some as intimately as bites.

All are so proud of their many legs
and their shells harder than yours
but which still engage their special part of outside
even if hiding from it in little caves or on the wind.

You are jealous of their certainty
that each knows what they are about.

But like you
they're movement and mouth.

35

You found out no-one's named all
the bacteria which live on this planet
nor even found the names
they call themselves,
skins over single cells.

If you cannot call it,
it doesn't exist.

Except that it has a million twins
and if number overcomes namelessness,
how do you include it here,
who it is, its life
lived in yours?

36

Somewhere in that cloud
is a water molecule from your tear
and in the wind, the carbon dioxide of your sigh.

Thus all nature vibrates
with you, or at least your ambition.

But it could be water from piss or sweat
or the exhalation of your angry yell.

You don't believe that, as your ambition
climbs the slipperiest walls
including that so smooth surface of time

you slide up, down, and along
comfortable as a clock.

37

The sun delivers yellow to leaves
knowing someone is at home
if somewhat sapped

by all the goings on which went,
including fruit, harvest, and the slow dry
that announces sometime soon

all will be cold and snow and dark.
Where you are, it's bright with the hope
that's realistic enough to know

somehow it's luxuriating in pretense
until it hits home. This moment
winter is somewhere else, but not now.

38

Rain is a short emblem of the clouds
which will liquefy and cover
three quarters of the planet
as each drop signifies a sea.

Rain on you stands in for tides and waves
and all that life and movement,
inviting but inimical.

How you long for beaches, paddling, surf
and yet can't survive in deeper than neck deep
as your head which desires
will drown in those clouds.

Breathe deeply, as you can, in the rain.

39

Arrogant sun insists on its light
and the earth, unable to stand it
turns away

but keeps, as it might
enough warmth to survive
huddling under its atmosphere.

Thus your conclusion:
the light and heat that sun
delivers is exactly right

allowing you to live here.
Thus the sun's confidence
and the earth's sucking it all in.

That door closes and there's no window
just an anodized sheet of blank metal
grey wall for this shed which stores,

stores all things you need a moment
here and there or not yet come
or maybe never but not thrown away,

away behind that blank wall outside
but written on its inside with the words
of things not needed now but kept,

kept against the imagined day
the memory index says yes there is
a thing you now need. Open that door.

41

Your body absorbs a blow
makes a bruise
and the technicolour skin effect of it all.

How does it know it must heal?
The body is wiser than the brain
you carry to carry consciousness.

That other blow–
how small you are in the vastness of the ill-understood
–bruises permanently.

Or as permanently as you're going
to get, another ouch!
Your body goes on, at least for now.

42

You collect lesions and discolourations
for your dermatologist who pronounces:
this one to remove, that one harmless.

Keep the harmless
because it's just working on
what it's working on.

to prove perfection impossible
now that the glass of night has shattered
into its countless shards of stars

which still suggest sense in it all
whatever sense may be
coming at you through your skin.

43

As the true skin of iron is rust
your skin discovers colour with time.

It still holds, as it must, all of you inside
and still touches the world

and all the sensation you think
is the world, but you're blotched by all that

and your living place
has also lost its smoothness
there a growth, here a shrink

but still and mostly
passing into dust
but a dust that's travelled.

44

Start on the footing that your footing
is solid, whether rubber-soled
or the surface of a planet spinning makes stable.

You might consider the danger of slippage
of a sudden stop, the hand on the brake

and it's gone

as no one steadies the foot of the ladder
you think you're climbing
and there's a slip

a whip back to ground
feet, hips, back and a whiplashed
head which held it all, you thought.

45

You navigate mapless
hoping to rely on an innate directional sense.

But you're so often turned around
by the dizziness of impulse.

Yes, it's windy out there.
You can tell by the way the clouds converse with each
    other.

But you continue to look up as if the sky
had answers when the only thing it has to say
is drowned out by that chatter of wind and cloud.

It's hard to bear, having no bearings.
You sometimes refuse to go
out-of-doors where it's so bright.

Your yellow car slides on the icy road
and turns its driver
upside-down
seat-belted
below the still spinning wheels.

The wheels slowly come to the same rest
as the car.

Snow might be falling by the time
the sirens and flashing red-lights arrive.

You now know
there are so many ways to find peace.

Traveling might be one of them.

47

A duck drags its "V" through the water
and then, a discreet splash and disappearance

and all is left to the glide of your canoe
and the pockmarks dripped from your paddle.

The canoe keeps you up on this surface
which might be a lake or simply all there is

except things come up
whether diving ducks
or fear of drowning
or the simple knowledge

it's just a lake just a canoe
and you're paddling as quietly as you can.

48

You might walk with a limp and mock the level earth
or this earth made level as machinery makes.

And your eyesight could be bad the stars so fuzzy
in their translucent sky there's no point in looking up.

Tension may tighten its headache concentrating inward
and away from the landscape so carefully placed around.

And the synapses might misfire wobbling logic to the point
there's no longer any point reason measuring nought.

If everything tends to zero
that other side of numbers,
the dust beyond comprehension,
what could you do as it does?

49

The night makes its noise.

A horn between the railroad tracks
rigid with insomnia,

a siren announcing
something incurable,

a dog's bark protecting
its upholstered den,

a moan from
a creature comfortable with computers
but still on watch for a predator's teeth,

and a scraping sound, gravelly,
removing that last layer of dark to reveal your day.

50

Evaluate the sunset
on a grade of orange and red
and the issue of descent.

Executed expertly
in the face of cloud interference.

It's a skill
the way the sun does this every day
projecting assurance

but still pronouncing the difficulty
of heaving the earth around
its colour changes.

Pass it this time and promote to the next.

51

The supermarket fills the empty space
of art with things to choose.

Stars, in the flicker of glass
containers scintillating white,
shine down and buzz and sing.
Pale faces open.

You will pick this and that
and leave the rest and smile and pay
with the usual electrons.

Everything thus dances down that empty space,
lines and beeps in common time.

Something you do.

52

Stepping outside you find it's true
the rain predicted now floating
on the hard surface of the planet.

It's all collected for return
wind, sun, transpiration
and all the other thirsts
which drive the planet–

you stay outside
let yourself get damp
as rain also returns through you
inelegantly, inexactly
made of water as you are.

53

You decide. There's A, B
and a bunch of alphabet
and then a letter you chose, option U.

Perhaps it trickled up from the subterranean
rooms which hold your thought's furniture
where there's leaky plumbing
and thus this, your decision.

You pretend you made the decision,
a straw and mud pie slapped smooth
from hand to hand until you're ready

and can announce, this clay
which looks like you, is.

54

In this, you're a dog
sniffing blades of grass and fence-posts
all of it so interesting, but what does it mean?

You have neither map nor memory
but know this is your corner
of all that is and you need to know
who else has announced this
and you'll sniff and consider.

You consider this the spot you are
and that moment's thought makes it yours
superimposed on all those others
unknown, but who are also here.

55

A bird flies its gold from the ground
to the branch where it can stand
shaded by leaf and watching you

watch it now calm after
the dazzle of its quick flight.
Not noticed until it moved.

You can only think it faces a life
as short as that flight from ground
to sky to branch

under a name you give it
like feather or bone or tidy
so neat is its quick departure.

56

An ant scurries into the canyon
of a sidewalk crack
and escapes the calamity
which is your foot.

Must all movement thus be
disaster for someone or thing?

Or only for those who can't get out
of the way

or can't get out of it at all,
including you, stuck in movement
as that's all you are.

Breathe deeply, walk on.

57

The pine needles tend downward
acknowledging the earth which informs them
of the goings on of minerals and water.

In this they turn from the sun,
which might explain their own darkness
or the darkness of the shadow they make

the saddening of light it is.
So, it's possible under pine
and its compact life

to know that life contains so much
earth and so much death which
after all, gives us back to earth.

58

An insect–
a millimeter's hard shell–
might crawl up this page
and over these words
not noticing it was not on leaf, bark or rock.

It walks its six unenquiring legs
to the edge of the page
missing that the words were about it
and its journey over them.

In this, that insect, nameless to me
perhaps not even in fact an insect
unfairly incites my jealousy.

59

Smoke drifts into the HVAC
of the sealed office towers and hotels

and there's a moment of panic
as the deal which imprisons
in this air-tight cell breaks.

You had believed in clean breathing
but it's a trap where there's no lifting the spring.

Best to be ignorant
and breathe as if it were
the most natural thing in the world

even as somewhere outside
a warehouse burns for the insurance.

60

The shadow falls over you
cold and dark like the fall of everything
this season

from leaves to frozen grass
and now the sun, lower and rising
only to fall.

The opacity which made that shadow
may be branch or brick
or mountain

but you know it's something immovable
until a quick turning away
and the sun outlines you on your ground.

61

Like all these plants, you find
the garden a place to sit
as you trespass on lawn

until you disturb yourself with doing.
Obligations flower in the sun
and the need to do, and find things done,

and confirm consciousness
while a rose is sure
it can do nothing
but make itself

go on. If that rose could make
a leopard, it would understand.

You could have done it differently
but don't know.

A rock, no matter how intensely
it wants to be an eagle
cannot make its crystals fly.

You might have chosen differently
for a different what's now.
(Better, you mean.)

This is merely hope
because in the end you run aground
perhaps against that rock
which aimed at eagle.

63

The clouds are tense–
you can tell by the way they bunch up and frown.

It might just be cold up there
but what they see below is hard and bumpy.

So many spires and trees
and inimical things upright.

The sky is reckless, allowing itself
to fill with these flighty things
which will break down soon enough
scared of the wind,
scared of heights,
scared of falling.

64

Make do with the presented facts.
A drought, a thunderstorm
are merely different kinds of thirst

as thirst itself can be lighter than air
or heavier than granite.

Having got this far, you wonder
why so much water and oxygen?
Present, that is.

Why this level, this much
and getting by, making do as it is?

So breathe and drink in the only real question
which is why can there be any question.

65

A stone investigates your fingers
turning glossy and damp
with the encounter

as its crystals run across
something less hard
than themselves
and fail to understand

as nothing with moist skin
has facets to catch and
flip light back.

And you would not
invite such things in.

66

You are cursed by understanding what's going on,
which is that you understand
you cannot understand what's going on
when everything else around seems to.

Rain finds its way down
the seed locates its tree
and thousands of unthinking
(you think) kinds of insects
find the cracks in the planet
where they can live.

For you, that's all in your head

and that's all your head has.

67

You've been given this time
you don't know how much
but you've had the left side of it
since you began.

There's a right side coming
but then the end and you
don't know how far from now
and don't want to know,
which is OK, because you never will.

There's a beginning and end for you
and another of each which stretches
from then to you don't know when.

68

You celebrate each birthday
by subtracting a year.

You have worked so hard
and perfected foresight of the day
your electric nerves will short out
blood cool and your cells
begin their descent to dust.

And dust to atoms to quarks
to black and then nothing at all
until again a galaxy.

You find yourself blowing out
fewer and fewer candles, and stars.

69

Yours is a pervious skin
through which all outside gets
colour and fragrance

idea and memory
no place softer for all places
but this within.

It's not just the entry
although it starts numerous things
and then their next, next, and next

until outside has made its way
to an inner story
that only that outside brought in.

70

You speak two Englishes.

One is long and latinate and legal
and something in the way
the will of the world
gets imposed.

The other is short, abrupt Anglo-Saxon
and meaning comes plain as bleeding
or having a shower.

Your ambition subverted or ambition suppressed
and it's a madness either way which does not wash

as you're so stained by how you live
and where and who tells it.

71

You're concerned about who's watching you
and what you think they're thinking
as they watch.

The pity of it is the watchers
may see a landscape which includes you
but what they're thinking about
is not you.

Pity, because standing by
is an entirety for you to see.

There, an electron's distance
from your concern is the indifference
which is all the atoms not you.

The apparatus of thought
exists in such decrepit housing
a laboratory

of crumbling bones
aching muscles
and diminution by viruses
which that house
innocently enough invites in.

But that's just you.

And all that great employment
which you think
is you.

73

You never know how it happens
not even after, how you fell
through the water and down

out of control, but still breathing
you are sure as you look around
at your dreams telling you stories

about people you know
all floating in this place
you also recognize, but can't name

until you come up for the air
you didn't know you were missing
and wake up, recalling only the fall.

74

You work with the idea that an idea
can be a mountain, or a tree
or that crawling speck

which sights the shadow that is
your foot coming down, and is no more.
Thus even your walking can be calamity.

So be it; it's only an idea
but what brought it along?
World-whelped, as you watched?

Or there, meaning there all the time
inside, surrounding, and merely itself
because it's there?

75

It's just the scale of the thing
an electron in its quantum shell
and the shell which is
the outside of everything

or that everything's inside
and even that can't be assured

although you hope your skin
contains all your electrons
as jumpy as they are

to conclusions
even scaring you out of your skin
with their possibilities.

76

You do this to meet a schedule
and pass the time
until that time and place
you have on a list somewhere.

Except to be somewhere
perhaps suit and tied
it wouldn't matter
although you know time

is material
if untenantable

except that you're but a renter
this moment and, you hope, the next.

77

What next after the next what next?
Our clocks say that time is a sequence
running in order
to be in order.

But hop skip and jump
from one place to another
memory insists on taking
a bit here and a bit from there

all past, but out of sequence pasts,
as the cause of this effect
follows later.

You know, because it all happened to you.

The sequined thought catches
light this way, then that
then suddenly gone

as it disappears into the fabric
which holds still and is dark.
So bright, such a moment

an odd random turning this
which caught the light
and gave light

and your illusion
of yes it makes sense
but the sense which disappears.

You might join the tin-hat brigade
aluminium foil wrapping brain-waves
keeping them fresh as promised.

Nothing will come in
and nothing leaves

which is rather your point
that it's all so essential and precious
you need nothing more
and can stand nothing less.

You confirm what you know in writing
and send it out scrunched up
like this, like used foil.

This potion renders invisible
all watchers, as being unwatchable
perfects the watching.

That potion predicts lottery winners
and all the wealth that's unearned
but still paid for.

Another potion delivers truth
as liars spread out their sequential art.

Yet another potion invests
with power over all, through all, and perpetual.

A final potion of words lists the ingredients
you blend to make the others.

81

Thought stops before it ends
the train running out of tracks
before it reaches all its destinations.

Of course, this believes that following
A to B or any other alphabet
or plan, will reach somewhere.

Is the surrender delivered
to the conqueror the not making
the next step, or no step?

With each peace treaty
you learn a little, perhaps
that there's so much more.

82

You watch the traffic that is you
considering the world around
the transit which is you.

Things go back and forth
between you and the world
mostly words for what the world is

but every so often you find a road
you didn't expect, had seen on no map
and which, without signs,
leads you somewhere
into the traffic
and away.

83

This is the moment you see through it all
and know your need to apprehend
has paid off

but you are about to fall asleep
you're that calm and you decide
all things will
reappear

or have never gone, still outside
your eyes with those closing lids
and that slow brain
impossible to see
through.

84

In your dream the clowns
have all the window seats
and grimace at the clouds
with exaggerated goodbyes.

They're making fun
of all accomplishments
while shouting privacies
into cell-phones: it is that absurd.

You have no answer
as they mock and laugh
and turn it all into a big joke
in that final preparation for take-off.

Did you choose any of this
from the possibilities numberless
because you haven't counted?

It being smart not to count
as a way of finding yourself
such a fragment you don't count.

But there are numbers for all of it.
One of those numbers is infinite
being all the things you're not

and the other number is one
being what you are
just one.

Fire keeps its flame upright
as heat is most ambitious.

It will burn through so much
to get to where it wants to be
as where it is it is.

You can only stare.

It (and so you) will get excited
about electrons and measurement
and starting and stopping

and all the other things
heated and electric that go
into your brain and travel.

87

This is the instant which is.
On this line there's a forward and back
and a point between, which you think is you.

It all depends on you,
including the notion that it does not
the dimension of that point only as big as you.

Perhaps you're at the point when day becomes night,
and you hardly notice, until you find yourself nocturnal
big eyes, sonar ears
and a different place

in which you gain the advantage
of you, that point, that sleeping world.

88

You breathe mostly by accident
or it's automatic but thoughtless
because you can't see air.

But a moment's hold
and you understand how this part
of what's outside gets in
and is needed in.

It's a hint of the final black-out
when your most precious understandings fail
even though one of them is your knowledge
of air's gases and isn't that something
or all?

89

You manage to stay alive for this
the holding up of the head
so the eyes can focus on what they see

which is words
which may be ink or even profound
as being alive

still, but unstill
and sure there's something lacking
which may not be much, but is something

which is the point and must be managed
now as surely as those words
which might also, to your surprise, be alive.

90

You watch yourself naming things
as you find them, not find as in looking for
but coming to your attention.

It's a matter of where you aim your look
or what strikes your eye
or merely diverts it.

Your attention
span is limited
by so much gaudy and obvious

in your eye
as a speck of gold does not irritate
even though it's still but dust.

You eat your bread, thinking
sense, only sliced into flats as flat
as the idea that your body will churn

this thing of carbon, hydrogen, and oxygen
into apprehension of the mystery
which lead to the existence of it.

Not meaning soil, seed, water, and sun
and then flour, yeast, water again,
but meaning a loaf of bread

sitting here, hiding behind the idea
of itself, neither idea nor self understandable
except on the blade of the sharpest knife.

92

You bought the furniture
and arranged it just so
a bed to make a bedroom

a table to serve the kitchen
and a place to sit becomes your study.
The walls the furniture thus made

assemble into a house
and you walk out the door
to the garden the house planted

and the street it stretched out
to the city those streets assembled
and there, as horizon, all the rest.

93

Arrangements
fall apart
as events dissolve their sugars
in the simpler substances.

Occasionally, a precipitate
coats an insight
giving it
a surface and extra edges

as it forms the crystal
which is the chance
of a new event
where you, the traveller can rest.

94

Your body sleeps, and one day, forever.
What lives on?

The elements of stone and water
and elsewhere which are your planet.

There's plenty more, of course
that variety of form and thing
which gives rise to festival and belief.

It may as well all disappear for all the use
it is to you once you're gone

except that, alive and sensational,
you believe it will stay even with you.

You mean: stay, even without you.

95

You speak in metaphors
with lunch an intermission
and every trip for groceries a journey

and your dreams like butterflies
arise from their caterpillars
into heavenly sky.

It's all about hope there's more
and something different and above
or even sideways, or anywhere
outside and sure
as your death will be mere sleep.

But the maggots will still be busy at your bones.

In this dream you dream
that you are dreaming another dream
laid down, but rising

to a cloudy horizon.
Perhaps it is night
but that seems not to matter

with the accepted logic
on which your world now floats.
There might even be light

but you can see, that ascent
you're sure is up but not sure why–
that cloud confuses things.

97

You imagine yourself above clouds
or on the seafloor
or handling that hard marble
at the Earth's centre

all to find a place where you
and the planet can know each other.

You are convinced you are
all possibilities
and can make all possibilities real.

Thinking thus
nothing happens except there
where you made them.

Setting it out in words makes it so.
Sentences spin galaxies into existence.

Enough galaxies and you've got a universe
at least convincing enough
you know it's there.

This makes it infinite
but as you think up verbs for those sentences
you keep reaching the same point

among the infinite points there are
that the pause for punctuation
is you.

Among all those stars you made.

This is your end, free in a world
in which you make things happen.

You set the stars along the paths
you dream for them.

You pop electrons into their shells.

You make days and cockroaches.

You invent sound and turn it
into sirens and song.

You encourage the seed to try itself out and up,
leaves and shade, for which you make sun,

and, all that done,
you begin your greatest construction.